Also by Paul Hoover:

Hairpin Turns (Oink! Press, 1973)
Letter to Einstein Beginning Dear Albert (The Yellow Press, 1979)
Somebody Talks a Lot (The Yellow Press, 1982)
Nervous Songs (L'Epervier Press, 1986)

PAUL

IDEA

HOOVER

The Figures

Cover painting, "His Black Ambition," by Walter Robinson, 1986
Courtesy of Metro Pictures, New York City.
Some of these poems have appeared in *Mississippi Review,*
Epoch, Open Places, The Brooklyn Review, OINK!, *Chiaroscuro,*
Lips, and *New Directions.*
Thanks to the Illinois Arts Council, a state agency, and
to the National Endowment for the Arts for Artist Grants
in 1984 and 1986.

The Figures, Great Barrington, MA 01230
Distributed by *Small Press Distribution, Sun and Moon,*
Inland Book Company, Bookslinger, and *Segue.*
Publication of this book is supported by a grant from
the National Endowment for the Arts, Literature Program.
Typeset in 10 point Times Roman by The F. W. Roberts Company,
Belfast, Maine. Printed by West Coast Print Center
Copyright © 1987 by Paul Hoover
ISBN 0-935724-23-0

For Maxine, Koren, Julian, and Philip

Contents

Idea

If writing is lying, nothing is true,
and pressure is on the mind, not eye,
as if in a single sentence a thousand
phenomenal objects fled a single thought.
"I can't spell and I hate this job—lying down
with swans, which has a dangerous charm."

But that was paradise, and this is the charm
one has with snakes, by casting one true
eye. *Sue Barton, Student Nurse* is face down
on the bed. Behind her, the young doctor eyes
her shapely form, and love is green as thought.
He clings to her like words, grows old a thousand

times before he's in her head. A thousand
years from now, people will wonder if charm
was the object, moving through our thought
like a boat among these islands. We'll be true
to the future, dull historical facts written down
in a moment of anger. History closes its eyes

at the thought of all of us dying. I hope I
never do. It's nice to be here for a thousand
reasons, including money and love, and put down
"lead pipe cinch," the phrase, which charms
and mystifies. Its very music is true.
Love has a thousand lives when a thought

becomes a word. Composed or known, thought
is blind as ice, then we give it eyes.
Sometimes nothing is beautiful or true.
When I'm feeling that depressed, a thousand
honeymoons can't cheer me up or charm
the gods and muses. Thank goodness, anyway, down

is not a mood, but simply a direction, down
San Antonio way. Life was a dream, I thought,
but then it took on the useless charm
of a garden. It looked me in the eye
and told a beautiful lie—no, thousands—
but of all my pretty answers only one was true.

Apology for the Senses

Everyone needs a good excuse,
like "I was driving with closed eyes,
thinking about your beauty, and I didn't see
your husband sleeping on the road.
Sorry! It will never happen again."

People like such explanations.
They want to know how you goofed
and what improvements you've planned.

Like today. Any excuse will do
to smash your face in some flowers
or let the city fall on your head.
You lean in the mirror to say,
"You've been looking tired and ugly.
Why don't you rest for twenty years?"

Or you're walking this diving board
above a lush blue pool in somewhere like L.A.,
wearing high-heeled shoes,
sequined gown, and shades.
Everyone thinks you're Death
in an Ingmar Bergman movie.

It reminds you of that dream
where flying fish stuck to your body.
You wanted the moment to pass,
but when it did, you wanted it back again.

And probably it's better,
in spite of rite and desire,
not to stand in the aisle, objecting to the marriage.
Still, brides of the world forgive you.

Various lights, creations, and shapes
move through your life like tourists toward Arizona,
where they have ten names for blue:
Freddie's Blue, Pretty Girl Blue,
Under the Tongue and Censure.
It's the kind of blue you see on TV,
where a beautiful landscape widens the eye
like a cheap romance in a window.
You grow into the objects watched:
a wrinkled tree, a monument slouching.
You sit on the edge of your seat,
deep in the motive of art,
which is sad, and funny, and dumb,
but anyway there you are,
corrupting a leaf with your presence of mind,
for which you apologize.

Long History of the Short Poem

She dreamed they lived in Africa,
on a beautiful green savannah,
where they raised speckled apples
and owned a bright blue ladder.
Life was good and they were happy.
The following day, she knew,
they had to go on a trip
to buy some beautiful dirt,
the most beautiful dirt in the world!

This was a dream about money.

He dreamed he was lost in space,
floating around in a silver capsule,
and the name on his suit was Geezer.
Maybe he was old, the Geezer in Space or something.
He couldn't tell, since there wasn't a mirror,
just lots of fuzzy chrome.
All he could see was the tip of his nose,
which looked about the same.
The odd thing was, this music kept playing,
a black polka band or a white reggae group—
he couldn't tell the difference.
He also remembered thinking,
as he looked toward Saturn,
"If only I had a sister,
there would be nothing to fear."

This was a dream about courage.

She dreamed they owned an aquarium,
but in order to make it work
they had to put quarters in it,

like a Vibra-bed or TV set.
After they put one in,
the fish started moving again,
the water lights came on,
and the little mill in the corner,
with its plastic man in the doorway,
began to turn its wheel.

It was then, of course, they knew she was pregnant.

Compared to What

Here in California, where ants are crawling
all over my hand and trees are green for a reason
but I can't remember what, something flew into
Marsha's garden, hung strangely in the air
without apparently moving its wings. A death's

head moth, I think she said, but there for a while
it was the emanation of something otherworldly
like in a Forties movie where Biblical things
occur—Lionel Barrymore seized by an apple tree
into middle heaven. I forget the name of the movie,

but he thrashed around for awhile, and that was
impressive enough. When a bead of water thrills
all over the skillet, nothing else needs to happen
and you've had it for the rest of the day.
Where do you think you're going, says the teacher

sharply, who do you think you are? Honestly,
says another, I should have thought you were better.
All those heavenly strangers seem so familiar now.
A camera focuses, darkly, a river, with little
light suggestions, and the rest is fluorescent

New Jersey, where, singing into a bullhorn,
we achieve the lyrical moment, see the face
of Jesus Christ inside a bowl of Jello. It's like
when you stand in the grocery store and all
the specials are on, but no one's in the world.

Such is the state of metaphysics, late in the new
decade. This is the lovely valley above the ugly one.

Life compressed in language, sights compelled by sounds.
As if I were blind to the world, all my whole life long,
and then it came rushing at me, time and time again.

Innate Ideas

It's a serious business being yourself,
but nobody else would do it.
You walk around with neon hair,
do ninety in maybe an alley.
"Adventures do occur, but not punctually,"
says Mrs. Moore in the movie.
The statement is true, but she is a fool.

It's not very funny to be killed by a book.
Here is Exhibit A, says the judge,
the actual book, the active page.
(Official anger falls short of rage.)
Inside, the monster smiles at the woman
as he holds her over traffic,
but she is sad, and the plot is dumb.

Here are the windows all over town
where you traced your shape in paint.
What an egotist you are: sitting,
standing, lying down, flying.
Such behavior is very unpleasant.
But it's fine to stand on a highway,
in the center of Pennsylvania,
waiting for deer to cross.
It's great to be transparent.

Someone wrote, "Father is an ocean."
But he still watches television.
There's a wrinkled glow on the water
where figures move, strange and deep.
This puts him to sleep, like the smell of rain
and money and thunder, and that's a nice situation,

since he's not yours but the poem's
and nobody *has* to care.
It's just an amusing thought;
language completes no final estrangement,
seduction or arrangement.
You were born with this idea,
including all the words.

Urge

This is the language talking,
but this is also Paul.
Tonight his curses are soft on the air,
and he wants you to know.
He says if there are angels
they're reading instruction manuals
on how to start a car, how to comb their hair,
plus they've got their clothes on backwards,
so walking here is going there.

Paul says when wrestlers hug—no, struggle—
the issue isn't good or evil.
It's more like stupid and shrewd.
But who can tell the difference?
Certainly not the language.
There's lipstick on the window
where somebody started or ended a novel.
A blue car passes so slowly
you want to go over and kiss it.

Paul says: a ball-peen hammer,
wham! on the back of a hand.
He says there's a word in German
for "winning oneself to death."
Paul says lots of things,
but that doesn't mean we listen.
What we like are edges,
a lion sketched in a parlor
among "the furniture of the mind."
What I'm Going to Do, I Think
remains a consideration, later a moral lesson,
but tact gets into trouble

because it was too discreet.
That's how it goes, says the language,
its eyes perpetually moving
over a slide of thigh, rise of sky.
Deep enough? Will do.

The Speed of Thought

It goes a mile an hour,
like a car horn from the Fifties
drifting out between two stars.
You think and think. It's crazy.
This fast, with maybe a rock,
you could blunt a pair of scissors,
and then you get this postcard
from Used Shoes, Nova Scotia,
where your thoughts went on vacation
and are "having a marvelous time."
They stand near a perfectly wonderful
cliff, watching waves get monumental,
and all around is a rich clear green,
so tidy at a distance, but hopping
with fleas on closer inspection.
Here and there are patches of moss,
like something metallic that grows
only in footprints of robots.
Later, wine and dinner, some clever
repartee. They miss you and miss you, OK?

Here in New Jersey, you miss them, too.
You sit on the concrete steps,
in polka dots, on Easter Sunday,
like one of the famous triplets,
and your face is four years old,
brilliant in that way. Pessimists,
too, are often seen smiling
because they know they're right.
Sadness is a science. The family
counts all the money you'll make
inventing all the kinds. You think

about zinc all day, the substance
and the word. As Robert Musil wrote,
"The sum of reduced individuals
may well form a totality of genius."
It's not that you think too fast,
just slow enough, like rocks in mud.

After Juanita Garza

When the mind is mirror on mirror
it takes on the brilliant roar
of afternoon notions like wind or

trees in motion. It's terrific knowing
the world's a place, where, owing
to the language, a word like "wing"

means something and rain stutters
on the sidewalks and gardens, terse
as a man embarrassed, saying "Er"

and "Uh" a lot. But you never pretend
in matters of the tongue. You tend
toward melodrama, which always ends

with an elephant burning, as in a surrealist
dream—with money, of course, a realist,
in love with a German cellist. Das ist

das Ding, nicht wahr? Your life could charm
the gods, but they're easily confused. "Harms
and the man," they sing, tattoos on both arms.

Perils of the Form

A transparent woman, on a bench in a garden,
in a painting by Bazille, is little more
than a drawing. That's how she amazes.
But the flowers and grass around her,

even between her ribs, become the flesh
she isn't. I'm surprised to see her
this morning in her frame. Wind blows
from the scene to strike me in the eyes.

That's all. The ''empty parade'' of my feelings
is a kind of brinkmanship, like standing
too near a train. I'm too near a painting;
it lands inside my senses like a bloody valentine.

Others as Ourselves

In the movie about truth, a boy tied knots
in grass to honor the dead for all they did.
Later he got drunk and burned the village down.

That was the excitement. But when he opened his mouth,
boredom grew like a secret. You'd rather watch
a fish shivering in a stream, anything but his wisdom,

which turns you into a servant. A person can't be
too careful when it comes to the use of words,
and poetry is lies—that's what people think.

It wants to put you at ease with one or two
great words, like "oranges" and "birds."
It wants to make a scene where a Cadillac

sinks in the river, its radio still playing.
And maybe it's delightful, like a cheap suit
full of polkas, because of the truth it reveals.

A friend of ours once said, "I get so shy
when I'm angry." It wasn't true, of course,
since all along we imagined him there,

awkward and basically dear. We imagined his moods
as they became our words; felt the coldness of his stare
as he regarded us, who had the nerve to think him.

Memento Mori

On television this evening,
a man on fire walked straight ahead,
too amazed by his condition to act anything but normal.
Then a boy was seen to cry because his mother was killed,
but the crowd that gathered around him
stared more at the TV camera than at his usual tears.

The moral is, a camera makes things dead.
That's why, when photos are taken,
you turn your head in a blur.
Who's that smudge? people often ask,
page after page in the family album.

In the photograph of Andre the Giant,
he looks from a miniature window
at falling snow that yawns in his face.
It's beautiful and true, but you feel dirty watching.

It's odd, at the movies,
how people like to pass between the light and screen,
casting themselves on the wall,
and it's fun to join that group at the Falls,
to be the stranger slipping in,
third from the left, fourth row.

Here's a photo of your father facing a field of wheat.
Between a glance and stare,
its truth is seen and believed,
but the details are quietly angry.

Here's your basic scene on the lawn.
The shadows of the family point in your direction,

and yours points back at them.
You stagger around with the camera,
trying to fit them in,
but someone's head is always lopped,
or there's only a photo of feet.
The moment the shutter clicks,
you take your eye from the lens
to see if they're still there,
drifting out of their poses.
All day they go around frozen.

A pretty girl sits on a cannon
while her boyfriend takes her picture.
Some firemen are posing and smiling
in front of a burning house.

You're walking one of those halls
where the portraits of founders are found.
It's a little like running a gauntlet,
the way their eyes are sharply focused
on some detail on the opposite wall.

Tribal Item

At the video store,
I ask for *Lacombe, Lucien,*
the one where a maddening killer stops in the woods
to stare at a leaf for five or six minutes.

"We don't have it," says the clerk,
"but how do you spell it, like comb?"

I spell it, including the comma,
with slightly French overtones.
Then I call Louis Malle
as she grows smaller, leaving through curtains.
I stand around smug for a while,
among the screens with their faces:
Orson Welles as a mean little boy,
Joseph Cotton with a bottle of aspirin,
and here comes the clerk again.

"No way," she says, impressed with my knowledge.
"How about *The Conformist* instead?"

"You mean the one with what's his name
playing the saxophone inside a bombed-out house?"
She knows I mean Gene Hackman.

"No, that's *The Conversation,*
Coppola's last good movie.
The Conformist is Bertolucci."
She turns and points at a TV screen
where Jean Louis Trintignant
looks dark and gloomy
in the back of a black sedan.

"This looks familiar," I say,

"but I can't remember what happens next."
Each successive scene comes like a deja-vu:
"Oh, yeah. Oh, yeah. Oh, yeah."
Now three women are singing "One Little Fitty"
while he walks around in a booth.
This is the part, you can tell,
where he makes a pact with the devil:
"He becomes a Nazi, right?"

"It's the Fascists, not the Nazis," she says,
giving the ceiling a who-is-this look.

"That's what I meant," I insist.
"It's Italy in the Forties,
and Dominique Sanda loses her family."

"That was *The Garden of the Finzi-Continis.*"
Her smile, I see, is a wedge,
like Babs on *The Life of Riley.*

"Let me see . . . *The Conformist.*
Is this the one where he gets her in bed
while the family talks in the neighboring room?"

"That's the one," she says,
mouthing the words like I'm deaf,
"but it was her husband instead."
Now I'm shrinking like a train;
I'm very far away, but out of some tunnel I say,
"Oh, sure. *The Conformist.* I've seen it,"
and as she turns back to her work,
I stand among these video faces,
which show by their look of dark concern
how incredibly vain and foolish I am,
unlike Lucien Lacombe, who grew at least in his movie
from a killer of chickens to a starer at leaves.

Maudlin Confession

When no one's around,
I like to turn the radio on
and listen for fifteen minutes
to sentimental songs.
Their emotional range is small
but satisfies some need,
and I stand there awed by the mediocrity
that cures me of existence.
It's also fun to look at mountains,
their cheap but massive grandeur,
and clouds have a visual candor
that's very appealing, really.
Such sights are comfort and consolation,
therefore somewhat corny.
Anyway, I like them.
Today, in a phone conversation
lasting about three hours,
Doris and I agreed that, given the right ambition,
a philosopher might succeed
without a single idea, and at the most,
like anyone else, needs only two or three.
I like the word "ambition,"
since it contains the world,
and I like what the barber said
when we were discussing poems:
"To write a poem," he said,
"you have to like life, I guess."
That's it, absolutely!
But then, to be a barber, staring at all that hair,
you have to like life, too.
Never mind that the cat just died
and the neighbors all sell insurance.

They're what Ted would call "ordinary terror."
So turn on the radio and let an awful song
run over you like a truck,
or read a little Traherne, who rhymes
"become" and "Tombe" with innocence and aplomb.
I highly recommend it,
though I wouldn't tell anyone.
It's what you do in private,
like counting your money and smiling,
and should end with a cigarette.

This About That

Anything can happen when it already has,
the way a word decays in your head
just before you say it. Anyway,
that's what I read, in a real or painted chair.
A shadow on metal sinks in like a scent:
three yellow cars, an orange van,
and a bread truck matching the leaves.
It's a visual rhyme a man now enters,
hurrying home in the damp. Nijinsky said,
"I like rhyme, because I myself am a rhyme."
It's like there's an object that wants to be you:
bowling ball, bushel of rice, the number nine.
To write, to wreathe, to writhe
and other declensions of turning—
ain't had a thought in days.
But Koren says Snow White sounds like Betty Boop,
and someone else says the truth,
of which she knows quite a little,
is like a translucent panel
that turns from side to side.
If I didn't talk to these people,
what wouldn't I know in life?
      Fornication, pre-marital sex,
      degradation, abomination, scurvy and lice,
      necrophilia, satanism, evil spirits,
      false gods, proud boasts and blasphemies,
      excessive stimulation, lower back pain,
      eloquence, threats, prime-time viewing,
      the light of our days, stardust, autumn leaves,
      and the theme of rain in the street,
from which sight rises like steam
e'en as I speak, which I don't.

I sit like the guy on the bus
who stares through the window like a porthole in space,
then turns and kisses your mouth.
Both of us sit there blinking,
as if it couldn't have happened.

Written on Songs by Lawes

While hearing this fairly beautiful music
by William not Henry Lawes,
I turn like smoke from a car on fire
and sag and wave for a while—
that is, well, sort of wave.
Other more natural beauties
stick to their several trees, so, while Lawes insinuates
a block of ice in a river that floats to sea and melts,
I walk around inside a thread of winter,
more refreshed than ever. Nothing is brutally dull,
like a dynamited pond on which the fish are floating.
Everything's very exciting, or moderately exciting,
or average at the least. Anyway, it's not dull.
Clouds, which looked at first like tumors,
become a shape and color both visible and able.
In other words, they're clouds,
just ordinary clouds, and rather attractive, too.
The music itches with complications,
packs itself like knives in ice . . .
    a voice, then no voice, beauty,
    or what we often call beauty—
you know how it is.

What Can Be Shown, Cannot Be Said

I sit in the almost-dark, as if at a movie,
writing notes on a pad, and it seems
there's flickering light in my head
where characters move like spooks,
taking shape and dissolving,
whole scenes shrinking like towns
glimpsed in a rear-view mirror.
I don't live in a hole in the ground
with a lamp, a chair, and some books,
thinking things into being.
I have a window to watch the clouds like pigs,
see falling snow grotesque what it hits.
An unblinking grammar of shapes
enters the mind like a storm
and sleeps in the nerves like a bum.
Kinda wish you'd been there,
between a blur and that thing there,
the thickest kiss, innate ideas,
and a neon sign that reads: EAT DIRT CHEAP
since that's the name of the place.

The Orphanage Florist

At the Angel Guardian
Orphanage Florist, I saw
flowers blooming in the

middle of the winter,
five degrees below. They
troped against the window

in order to get
more light and wound
up frozen to it

(the window, not the
light). I also saw
a truck, blue against

the snow, on which
the name was written:
Angel Guardian Orphanage Florist.

It passes through the
streets as something totally
real. I'd thrill to

see it coming with
birds of paradise or
orchids for the prom

opening fertile petals, the
moist buds thrusting out.
Stevens said, "Death is

the mother of beauty."
I don't believe that
yet. A blue truck

on some snow, that
is the mother of
something, call it beauty

then. The neighborhood contains
the Midwest Mambo Club
and two stores named

Hosanna. The School of
Metaphysics used to be
located over Harry's Bar,

but now it's somewhere
else, behind an orange
door, some kind of

scam, no doubt. I'm
mental enough already, beetle
brow on fire with

momentary truth, grace to
stay alive, which takes
attention given. For seven

seconds once, I had
ambition fever, wanted to
be the thee, the

the for whom a
crowd would wait like
nervous mice, but that

was not the answer,
cancer of the heart.
"The Botticellian Trees" by

William Carlos Williams sends
its "ifs of color,"
delighting the very hair,

but word for word
for word, from glass
to light to flowers.

Some Polonius

The practice of burning witches has been discontinued
in the New England states. With notable exceptions,
sexual activities occur during evening hours
and in the privacy of the home. Trees falling
in the wrong direction may smash a line of cars
and take the lumberman's life. A bull calling
in a valley evokes a note of sadness, and things
in general happen which may be hard to predict.
A sidewalk over a ditch reveals a troll beneath.
When lights are on in an attic, they often shine
in the basement, too, but never in other rooms.
The Green Mill Bar and Grill will continue
under that name. The Ramar of the Jungle
Shopping Center and Mall must undergo renovations.
Bargains may be obtained by comparing prices
and weights, but a cheaply purchased product
may unravel or stall, and you'll have to find
a replacement. The train you board today
may be headed in the wrong direction, resulting
in trouble tomorrow. In the story of Prince Hamlet
it is natural to sympathize with the plight of Polonius.
Fathers should not be stabbed, even when eavesdropping.
The ability to count your money is a matter
of importance but requires no spiritual knowledge.
Time is often compared to moving water.
Time and money may both be "spent," but one
can step in his money the same time every day.
Opinions are known to vary on a large number of issues.
You are wise to temper yours so as not to be caught
in foolish posturing. A garden should be planted
some time in the spring and harvested in fall.
Asparagus continues its subterranean way
no matter how often you cut it.
German food is heavy but not without some taste.

English food lacks spice, and French food is renowned
for its clever preparation. The opera by Ravel,
L'Enfant et les Sortilèges, is a privilege to the ear
and contains exciting moments that will draw you
out of your chair. Never give your name as Maurice
in a country and western bar. Italians from Parma
are severe in their judgment of song.
A cruise at sea is entertaining for the first
two days or so. Thereafter you may be bored
and spend your time in the cabin, shades pulled
against the light. Playing ping-pong at sea
can result in loss of the ball, and frequent shifts
of wind challenge the skill of the players.
Shuffleboard is a stabler game, as the wooden tablets
keep a tentative hold on the deck. "Thrust" is a word
used in discussions of sex and the power of motor cars.
Miles per gallon may be ascertained by dividing
the miles by the gallons. Always ask permission
when staying overnight on Indian reservations.
Do not start fires in a forest. A great hazard
is presented to the animals and trees, and smoke
pollutes the air you had come to enjoy.
Whatever you do, try to do it well. It's sad
to waste your life. Find someone to consult
when things aren't going your way. It might cheer you up,
and lively conversation is a pleasure of its own.
Smooth surfaces are best for bowling alleys
and roller rinks. The death of a parent
creates a sense of loss. Dares are foolish to take,
particularly if offered by enemies of long-standing.
The lookdown is a narrow fish possessing a steep profile
and mile-high eyes in a hatchet head.
Pride is a common failing and next to gluttony
the most serious. When escaping from jail,
look carefully before dashing into an open space.
There may be a guard with a gun who's eager
to do you harm. When fighting with a knife,

wrap one arm in cloth to prevent its injury.
It is also a good idea to move quickly on your feet.
When driving a motor car over railroad tracks,
do not linger too long. The same may be said
of standing, as the force of the powerful object
may draw you under its wheels. The teacher's apple
should contain no worms. Some children actually jump
over candlesticks, but finding your way home by dropping
crumbs in a forest is very difficult. Try, try again,
but if you don't succeed after several years,
consider some new project. Cover your mouth and nose
while sneezing, and do not tuck the tablecloth
under your belt when dining. Natives of San Francisco
never call it "Frisco." Cincinnati is not "Cincy."
Approximately eighty miles separate Dayton, Ohio,
and the capital of that state. Of all the names
of cities, Springfield is most common.
Postmen have early hours, but their work is fairly
pleasant. "Sheherazade" by Rimsky-Korsakov
is a dated composition, and figurative music
in general startles one into a laugh. Winter storms
and pastoral calm show the most contrast, while flutes
and violins should represent babbling brooks
and flight. The cello is melancholy, the oboe sly.
A number of small men wearing evening dress
invite comparison to Patagonian auks, also called penguins.
People who dress like swans must bear the consequences.
Of all the various cheeses, Swiss is the least pleasant,
followed by Velveeta, though either may be used
in the absence of other nutrition. Rotate your tires
every six months or so. Change the motor oil
every five thousand miles, more often in stressful climes.
Be temperate and kind, and if you stop to smell
the flowers, try not to be late for work.
It is good to please your boss, and be not acrimonious
in your dealings with fellow employees.
The Fresh Meadows Garbage Dump offers one example

of unconscious irony. From a few great words
a few great books may grow. Poems about hamburgers
are often humorous. Songs have simple phrases
and are usually known to rhyme. A small fire
may be extinguished with a single watermelon.
Mental health consists of appropriate behavior,
but the standard often varies from one culture
to another. Serving blubber for dinner
will not work out in Winnetka. The Platonist denies
the reality of sensation. Aristotelian thought
has its practical side. When taking your first plane ride,
sit along the aisle rather than by the window
and do not advise the pilot in the middle of a landing.
A Bloody Mary will cost two dollars. Beer is often less,
and soft drinks are usually free. Anxious situations,
like getting beat up in an alley, are often a source
of humor. Never believe, in life, that nothing
will work out. Your time is coming soon, so try
to be awake when the light erupts that means
heaven is yours on earth. Every acceptance speech
should show a hero's calm, a scholar's reserve,
as well as your heart-felt joy that this could ever happen.
Eighteen is the sum of three times five plus three.

Views of the Garden State Parkway

It's a series of painted photos,
the kind they made in the Forties:
tintype of a tollbooth, the Tuckerton Interchange
with overpassing local road, a roadside telephone booth
where a melancholy figure makes his evening call,
and some travelers having a picnic
in a "Typical Wayside Area"
while the foliage around them reddens and rusts.
Here the language veers, but not away,
since for all its pictures, continuous gifts,
and golfing psychology, it makes us genuine beings.
We are the watchers regressing into macadam and grass.
Somewhere, Baxter's theatrical scream
is muffled in curtains, and "jeepers" is a curse.
But here, quite simply, is a view of Raritan Bridge,
with an older bridge beside it
that's soon to fall in a muddle.
Even a timid person is vivid
in the mind of the object seen,
and it speaks him in return, the way that bridge
expresses the water beneath it.
In one of the photographs, the shadow of a cloud
drifts along with cars, but soon it leaves the road
and disappears over a hill.
In another, a man waves from his roadster,
as if he liked our essential being,
and it's like a dog in the park
that chases only shadows, not the things themselves.
Then many things seem to wave
with faithful regard and charm:
the gentleman at the window . . .
anxiety during polo . . . life as meaningless pageant.
But look at the reddening shadows of trees

impinging on the road. See the yellow field.
Consider the turbulent blue of the sky.
Meant, gestured, guessed, a philosophical sketch
of life on a traffic island means "here" and "I'm alive."
Nobody thinks it a crime on a road near Asbury Park.
Here's a bird's-eye view of Monmouth County.
Here's an interchange in the Pines.
That's all. Somewhere in closer detail
a doorbell rings and curtains part.
Someone is wrinkled and needing a drink,
hair like masses of cats.
Someone is pressed into walls, like a Vuillard
scene where mother knits herself
into worn wallpaper, and the orange on the table
is a moment of summer we'd rather see than eat.
Weather as precision . . . murder in purr.
But here, a violent flirtation, the way an adjective might,
and photos spread out like days, simply points of view.

Heart of Darkness

The flowers in the carpet the color
of blood remind me of the helmsman
in Conrad's famous story. He clutched
the spear as if he cherished it, and
his face toyed with a frown. It's
a beautiful tale about madness and
death, and I heartily recommend it
after you've finished *I Love Lucy,*
which images in its humor the loveliness
we feel. Then there was *The Life of
Riley*. Gillis, the next-door neighbor,
stood with William Bendix beneath a wing
at Boeing, riveting and gabbing. The
main theme seemed to be what sandwich
Babs had packed—not the sort of show
in which the mirror bleeds, no helmsman
on the floor. Add Pinky Lee to fifty
bucks and you get a million years
compact as dust on shelves. Backwards
we would say, "Sadness of note evokes,
returned has drollness and," but the
tether drops the bell in one of our
miscantations, and that's a speech
that fails beneath the skirt of thought.
The heart of darkness is a bull on fire
in a valley, giraffe lost in an alley.
Won't someone hire poor Pinky Lee?
He's dying to come back. But, no,
he just recedes like Kurtz's cry in
the jungle. While Marlow throws his
shoes in the river, Pinky stares at
a grey television which gives a little heat.

But make mine fascination. When I think
about the past, it's always in technical
French, and charts are spread in rooms
in the antique light of seeing. There's
an object on the table no one recognizes,
then a word is found for it, like Apache
lemonade. The dictionary says, "neglect
in reporting a crime." So I pass this
cogitation to you in object glass, and
you guess who I am through schemes of
"the" and "and." Extracted from blue
and desire, we both require a style
part obelisk, part reminder: to be
an O.B.E., a sterner obiter dictum.
Grim as chromosomes, we line up for
a cakewalk that leads to our division
into you and me. The world is stained
by gazes to which each thought adheres
like a pink tongue to a post, and the eye
rocks in its socket as it follows the
bouncing ball: thin, thin, thin. No
meaning overall, just a thing that
happened, the star boarder's frivolous
comments in a well-ferned anteroom
fictitious as horizons. (They recede
as we get nearer.) The whole exchange
revolves on a fondness for amusement.
Plants rise in their delight that something
stirred them up, and I pour myself on you
with modesty and restraint in spite of
an arrogant gift that frames you like
a portrait of Juan Benito Juarez, neither
man nor words. This means: I will kill
you. Then: Your brother will kill me.
When the silent actress lifts her face
to the light, it erases her Byzantine
features. Everyone stares at the sky
where the Paraclete parachutes, his thin

Einsteinian hair making an aura of words.

It reminds me of a dogfight above Danville,
Ohio. The planes got mixed together, and both
came blinking down. One pilot floated into
his own backyard, but the other was strapped
to his seat and landed face-first in a field.
We ran around with our hands in the air,
glad, almost, it happened, for those were
the days when people would run from their
houses to watch a jet go over: father with
half his mustache and a shaving mug in hand,
mother with a plate of liver she was going
to inflict on the kids. Isn't it odd, I used
to think, that everything has a name? That
jet could be "banana" for all the language
knows, and the back of the knee has a title
which means "a clear philosophical view."
Each word attends its picture then fades like
a painterly trait: the apple with its curves,
light that shines like baldness. The memoir
of a *thing* is given in the open, like the
sponge of Francis Ponge, and its character
grows to a bold seduction. Yellower by
the minute, the eye becomes the lemon
reflected on its surface, and in spite of
an imminent shrug, I'm with it in the effort.
Language is a strafing run in no particular
line, proceeding from A to B through every
other point, of which I may be one, hulking
light of mind erasing as it goes. "Declamatory
unison of the whole band"? My dear, it's
raining pianists and plastic bowling trophies
with small bent men on top. It's pretty
heroic, though, how they hold the ball
like Zeno's arrow between this point and that,
neither leaving nor arriving but just plain
gathering dust: the French, the horn,

the leave, the tree, the shore, the toast,
the knot, the seam, the telephone, and
window. Blue creates the air. Green
is rather convincing. We get back Bach
in splinters, and saying turns its head
like an agitated mantis that hears its prey
approaching—low cries among the singers
consisting of General Song and the Chinese
Gongsters, a canto interruptus. Wavering
folds a father flag where can't pretend
is heights, and I shoot the barest step
one-tenth of one percent, since up
is in that realm, clear to hear the sibyl
drink a fascinating hand. It's a Poulenc
glass landscape. Widened in a face, collapsing
in the frame, there's now and then some fun
they tend to put on bread. A B-flat cat
on rat arranges rightness twenty-six
times three. Storms Pound Coast.

Which brings us to our theme, bright as
Indianapolis in a wincing summer rain.
I'd like to tie it up with a neat little
bow of darkness, bring back bony Kurtz
with his loss of words at the end. Not
a man as much as a place, he's sane as
Jimmy Stewart giving a worried look whenever
someone hugs him. He confesses to rolling
apples to see which way they lurch. It
cures him every time the light shakes through
a parrot's cage, and a sumptuous run on drums
wavers thoughtlessly, each note a dazzling
subject with endless variations on what
had seemed a plan. He loves the Edward
R. Murrow slouch of a city street. Are
landscapes more than acts? The plain
is very plain. He may say he never, but then
he finds he has, repeatedly and with meaning.

After Cotton Mather

It's cold and rainy now. The baseball
game is off and friends are moving out
of town as jealousy sets in, but this
is where it's done, not Boston or Hong
Kong. Sophomore psychology keeps me
in the dumps no matter where I live,
as Kenward E. suggests in a letter re:
my slump. That's gone now, thank God,
and drollness has returned, the Wally
Cox routine. A man in the street exhorts,
"You know me, I'm real" even though he's not,
having disappeared in car-on-pavement noise.
When Darlene's father died, the family
put dice in his coat so he'd be buried
with them. In Vegas as in heaven?
The Kaddish made me weep though I didn't
know a word. The rabbi said Howard kept
the family fed, and the *kindele* stayed
together in spite of difficulties too
numerous to name. As Koren says, "It's
one bad life to another," blue-eyed
pessimist stuck in second grade. It's
Chaos Day, September 21, and her spelling
words include "little," "winter," and "still,"
which catch my mood like a letter that stands
on edge. Pride, gluttony, eagerness, avarice,
and lust: It's a good idea, kids, to practice
them all at once, but please don't tell your
parents who gave you this advice. Signed,
the man in the overcoat.

　　　　　　　　We wanted to talk
like gods, but how do our gods talk, comprising

Tony Lestina and tuna patty melt? "Oh, yeah?"
and "So what!" are among the sounds we hear
on a furtive pink sand island in one of the
neighborhoods. How to say politely, "Get out
my face before I kill your ass"? Maybe there
ain't no way, but one is brought to passion
because the Cubs have lost, as they very well
think they must: "It must have been the shadows,
dear, falling over the field." "And I'm Marie
Antoinette," comes the quick sarcasm like rain
on a tin-roof house. Whispering into the language,
the edge of talk itself touches tongue to thought.
We stand by as observers in the spoken forward
movement of exactly what we are, something
mumbled through a wall like prisoners saying
goodnight, and again there's the sound of wind
leaving a trace of itself.

                              Soon we're having
a party, and a cake will have to be ordered.
Last year the Russian baker, not knowing English
well, wrote in a kind of jelly, "Happy Dearthday,
Koren." I was the furious parent explaining
the meaning of words, but he couldn't change
the script. We ate the dearthday cake, danced
and sang like swells. Now I am here in words,
and you are there in words, shaped in the mind
like bells. It's nice to think outdoors, where
North and South collide inside a candy wrapper
and the clarity of the landscape simply lies
there endless, a pattern of rises and curves
in theoretical weather. We sit in the shadow
of a narrow sandstone scarp, gazing at the heat
that changes shadow edges. We garden the place
with thought, author ourselves within it as in
a summer palace where furious yellow birds
enhance the past with speed.

An errand into
the wilderness brings us to the suburbs where
houses sit apart with picture windows blazing.
"In a word, take the meanest Saint that ever
breathed on earth, and the greatest scholler,
for outward part, and learning, and reach,
and policie, the meanest ignorant soule knows
and understands more of grace and mercy than
all the wisest and learnedest in the world."
Or the other way around. Light still strikes
the leaf. Moisture finds the root. At the
little Christian college where I found myself
enrolled, they had an annual Maypole dance:
four fairly virgin lasses, barefoot on moist
soil, winding the phallus with ribbons, blushing
with exertion near the tennis courts. In the
hallways of the campus, founders of this very
thought were framed along one wall, stern men
with folded hands and hair like combed meringue.
The song begins with a story and winds up flat
on its back, indefinite decisions creating
hesitations like towers of picnic baskets
at the edge of autumn rain calm as knives
in ice: "among" as not "between," "either"
turning to "ether," a long row on the lake
that tensed to be a stream, the flatness
of the sky against the curve of earth,
the bloom of life in dots, a woman trailing
her hair in a perpetual glimmer of water.

Subject Matter

My Mind to Me a Kingdom Is.
It shapes a mind in the eye.
Name three things wrong with the picture.
        Dear Hoover. Removable labels.
"Needless to say, I'm back in the city,
Back at gym and school, and eating out
in restaurants with good friends
almost every night, and it's not a bad life."
                Am weather
as precision, *Afternoon of a Bellhop,*
out from Angleton, Texas. A black car
        enters the gaudy pagoda & I of course
        am a fool. Who heard a bad man say,
        "rarely rare"—that's good.

Anybody knows. Loveable old phonies
who own a geyser and charge you to see it.
Between the word and its object,
the things we used to say,
like jazz when it meant fuck,
that girl she sure had spunk,
Lo, it is written. La Banana. In a coma.

            a song overheard
        some unrevelation
                and what nice weather we're having
        I tell you this
                as a beast of the field
        If momently the world
                a bowl of lemons
        just a pure plain song
                inwardly thinking Not
        sincerely yours
                Montgomery Ward & Yale

safes are sagely falling
        brides from cakes
cities from maps
        I tell you this
like a house arriving
        what darling feet
thick reading
        kneeling among
What a monster you are!
        excellent bringing
exacting eyes
        Morris Whoosis
Milton Average
        embarrassed to be dancing
In weather, of course, it's work,
a ship of evening hours:
        "We will pay only a limited benefit
        if the insured commits suicide,
        while sane or insane,
        within two years from the policy date—
        see Specified Amount."

Snow falls onto moving water,
leaving a blur on the surface.
Po Chi stares at the river
from his horse on the icy bank
and ponders the nature of beauty.
Perhaps it is fullness, he thinks,
or the meeting of two moving things,
or death, or slowness, or seeing . . .
        His mind fills up with these things.

        "Here is an anthology of the best poetry
        of the Vietnam generation: Ohio farmboys
        in faraway jungles with unfamiliar names . . ."

Names like Locke and Leibniz:
"Since it is impossible to think distinctly

and at once of everything we know . . ."
Since a thought is always prose,
  the mud and various grasses,
  adolescence, Pennsylvania,
  quantity, price, discount, total.

  Has modernism failed?
The incarnation of Mortimer Snerd,
which I myself desired,
  & these attractive errors
  seem written at first in German;
  hands and tongue go numb,
  rivers of intentions.
It's leaving your mouth where you kissed,
the lingering smoke in a room.
  I would be (I was) embarrassed.
  Hwaet! Its feet.
Chaucer, said David, is flying.
Then the other David said,
  "Fond of leather
  and the smell of damp wool."

Sweet to be in pieces.
Very solid, great, and real—its bedrock concerns
like the sky, *Just Above My Head.*
The heavens shall glow, but I'm not excited.
I lie around in my suit of suet, earth, and worms.
  Long pause. Violins.

Twins in Mirror

Whenever I see New Haven, I often say
New Heaven. I haven't seen "New Haven."
  When an error
  is made
backspace to the error. The error is now
removed. He worked at making mirrors.
  Sometimes they
  would break,
and pieces of the factory would lie
around composed. In a cotton dress,
  I always
  imagine "her,"
of which he was a member, and does
her father remember? Let no word disdain
  with dials
  of mother
of pearl while the moon shines on the hood,
creating a lake of metal. The Rhondas,
  Push-up Bras
  or simply
Sam & Dave. The man sang "Mannish Boy."
Death reduces stress. In France was done
  by man
  with gun.
Therefore, in the end, he became Saint Slave
of Wages. As sung by Snooky Lanson.
  To deify
  the dog.
How beautiful is the yonder goddamn sofa,
as probably I desired, which thinks her
  into song
  and turns
to a life of adventure. After all, who don't?
To deaden the senses, which I rented for

          my daughter
          to rise in
social class. Then I'm the one out driving
what modesty forbids, the fade at ballad's
          end the
          color of
my eye. Here is the walking mirror
Flaubert called the hardness of her arms,
          in which
          a shape
takes place. Repeatedly as a child.
"The bowling ball also explained why plaster
          was always
          falling, huge
chunks the size of Texas, and why at night
we'd hear this tremendous thumping."
          We and
          our works
are mortgaged to die (see flashlight
under ice) but this is not to be spoken
          at 19
          Haldane
Terrace. When her brothers called her
into the yard, she saw the shadow arriving,
          as if
          to cut
her in two! On its way to Kansas City.
Five women are pictured holding a shark
          somewhere in
          Wisconsin.
Six boys easily fit inside the studio moon,
and they are happily smiling into the eye
          they mind.
          Believe you
me, if you put one hand in water, the other
in a socket, your words will come out slowly,
          that's what
          he said later.

Calm Song

It's seductive at first standing at the prow
of a ship caught fast in ice,
your crossing-the-Delaware tie gathering the breeze.
Then your teeth begin to ache
with smiling into the cold. Isn't that the way?
Muttering mounts a mansion
built with playing cards. Oops, there it goes again,
and if you take the local train,
localities lack color and no one waits at the station.
You'd hardly glance through dusty windows
at trees that look like spills. Bald men meditate
salads seen as maps. A brilliant seaming
leans to thinking, but then again not really,
the literal agent of grandly calling I can't.
You can't. So let's forget it, pal,
but call me once in a while, OK?
You have to stand a little at a time,
like small abstractions building an object.
Finally you arrive at song shapes grown on prose,
serenely serenade the tentative dream of sense.
The sign announces, "No Shoes, No Shirt, No Service."
Yes, that was the basis of it, everything taken aback.
You change your mind like blinking your eyes,
the self-sustaining question creating a logical space
the answer whittles down. You've played there
in the shadows, watching spiders rappel,
secured by the thread that drives them out,
and you've seen letters appear—Beth, Zed, Vav—
in the branches of a tree. Is everything what it seems?
Clouds move over the sea, imaged in the water.
Shadows ripple on dunes, and sections of a life
rise like musical stages with gleaming brass profound.
You feel it as it happens—statues on a truck,
transported from Newark to Nyack, fall at every turn.

Disorder, stay thy hand. You had not intended,
but he wishes and she has. That means implications
beyond our little praxis. The eye tracks through a frieze
shaken by the wind, and it's just the past again,
obstinate as a name, solid as a myth.
The novel began, "She had invited Ed but didn't recognize him
in the luxury of that group thick as a jeweler's eye.
Oh, she was richly aware, for though he dressed
like a king, suppose she didn't comply?
That would show them all!
Still, the porch was certainly pleasant
in the light that time of year, and it was amusing to sit,
with nothing to say, ever to have to say.
The future was hers alone, to razor, or not,
her clothes. It was undecidable.
Distance focused the window.
Dreary nothing ran up a flag."
Will there be anything else? Yes, and coffee later.
By what authority, not Sartre and Camus,
did he bring his soothing doctrine
to her reluctant damage? You try to boil it down
to an irreducible chaos like a vanishing bark at the door,
while dark night hides its cars in chillness,
drollness, nullness, dullness, shrillness,
illness, smallness, stillness.
Dear diary, comma, speaking of death, comma,
I am not a poem, but I said that before.
A ruined de la Tour? Scuffle in a zone?
The lemon on the table just made a brash assertion,
and I am a little flower.

Necessary Lie

As I was saying, before the wind
so rudely knocked me down,
each new truth leads to an ultimatum.
You can either stand for it
or get stampeded by it.
The old ones hold, of course,
like perfume down a dress
or bells that resonate ever so faintly now,
and they are what we are,
down to the bone and marrow.
New truths make new creatures,
but they're often charming monsters.
Each day, in a sense, plows under the offenses
of the one that came before.
This is nothing new, a truth you're proving now
by the very way you breathe,
like someone caught in an elevator
with the Muzak loudly playing—
and where do you think you're going,
on another brilliant errand
that takes a life to complete?
Sometimes, on the way to a truth,
beautiful words intervene,
as if they wanted to be in your life
like men in a motionless boat.
But the scenery's so amusing,
you frankly haven't the time
to be drawing one truth from another.
When the Pied Piper's led by rats,
the foolish sayings of a wise old man
serve as nervous comfort
while we sleep with pigs and dogs.
The matter's instinctively practiced—

you sort of know and don't.
In the middle of such knowledge,
as one friend hinted darkly,
I'm a tourist, not a spy,
and among a hundred drawings of daddies,
the one I've become will do.
I'm helpless in its presence,
so kindly comb my hair,
that nest of contradictions
that's equally there and not,
like sunlight in Vermont.
It's not a pleasant business
pinning these things down,
and reluctance is truth of its own.
A simple word like "though"
carries us from fact to shadow
in the running sweep of a clause.
"Green shelf upon green shelf,"
it slips away like land in the If and So
of clouds throwing light on hills
by not being there for the moment.
Impressed by that near-truth
in its brave simplicity,
we begin with a syntax of stones
arranged in a widening circle
later perceived as a house.

Sunlight in Vermont

After the circus we talk in our sleep.
"What is it?" we say, "What is it?"
and I think I know what we see:

an elephant sitting on haunches
like a baby after its bath
(it teetered above us with watery eyes).

And then there was Cincinnati,
the ancient clown with no sense of humor
who juggled surprisingly well.

No one could stand to watch him
in the half-deserted tent,
but, after all, we came for the pathos of it,

and every now and then
something great would happen.
The albino wearing the Gorgeous George wig

spat kerosene onto a fire
and rubbed flames on his arms.
We cried out in amazement,

for he snatched doves from the air,
a true and actual magic.
It's a lumpishly handsome world—

no "poverty of words,"
just a loveable charlatan
installing a small elation

like the warmth on your cheek after slapping.
With a mist in your head like a valley,
you search for the verbal excitement at fights,

and this too is a circus,
the crummier the better,
where a dog with rhinoceros skin,

"believed to be from China,"
can be seen for fifty cents.
For just a little more,

you can ride the elephant
around a baseball field,
swaying like a planet.

(We both realize,
as glances are exchanged
between the show and crowd,

that you coerce these words
to pose a satisfaction.
Between a hand and understanding,

our conversation gathers
like moths on a TV screen,
its being only phrasing,

something misheard in *MacBeth*
that later turns the plot
toward pleasant dreams and ease.)

2

Every five minutes today,
I rushed into the weather
to photograph a cloud

brushing the top of a mountain,
but the cosmic view from the side of a hill,
where we're entrenched with books,

is depressing after a while,
too remote for the mind to hold,
and the lens reduces the land,

can't smell the piney air,
feel wind pushing trees together.
Placing the photos in rows,

like Monet's lily pads,
reveals an empty obsession.
Yet the plain thing is enough,

and even more than we wanted,
a frivolous climate of *what*.
No characters float through

with characteristic manners,
mouths twisted in a thought
that will later cause them awe,

and why do I think of my face
as the sort of thing one finds
beneath his food on a cheap historical plate?

Today, to fight the loneliness here
and refusal of friends to love us,
I read a hundred pages of *Finnegans Wake*

and perfectly understood it!
Then Terry called from Lincoln, Nebraska,
to say he is getting divorced.

No such problems here.
We fight and get it over,
as one frog swallows another.

Last night's thunderstorm,
which wakened us into a daze,
continues to amaze us,

the clarity and length of sound
as it stumbled across the valley
like something made of rubber.

So, on the whole, it's too dramatic here,
the mountains presenting even farms
as something to consider,

Platonic cows that float in air.
I'd thrill for a lawn, that is;
turn my back to the window

with its saw-toothed mountain chain.
If you want to know,
Finnegans Wake is a prose meditation

in which Joyce justifies himself
not to God but to Ireland,
and it ends with a gracious nod

to his poor defeated father.
Thus ends my book report,
as the shade itself approaches,

not for a life but the evening,
attractively paratactic
like Baby Tuckoo sneezing.

Asleep in his mansion?
A shape in his man chin?
A sheep in his mention. Engines.

3

The "geologic opera" of hills reposing
should be a thought of its own,
quick as a continent shifting.

Today we climbed up Smuggler's Notch
where roads disappear in granite.
Maxine was wearing heels, and people

on the trail stared at her in amazement.
We were dressed for the shopping center,
not for the wilds they thought they were in.

At the top we found a stagnant pond
dammed by forest rangers
to look like a beaver had done it,

and I thought of Walden Pond
where Thoreau lived by Emerson's grace
while his mother did his laundry.

I'm glad it's used for swimming,
proud of radios playing Boston rock and roll.
But who am I to say it?

I'm about as involved in the matter
as smoke from an orange candle;
the memory of that opinion

is momentary air of which I am a part,
then we disappear together.
Each triangular leaf points in its own direction,

in and out of the light
where paths calm down to "nothing,"
if by that we mean ferns

growing in sturdy patches
and moments of green water
implying other life.

They amount to a story
that's simple enough in structure
but hard to understand,

arriving in pieces of this, that, then
that make a fretful presence
in the vacancy of an eye.

Subdued by the tension of years
stretching back to town,
I'm Joyce's "binocular man"

at the wrong end of the lens,
since that makes objects dear.
In the intervening mirror

reflecting cloud or ground,
there's a carpentered emptiness
often confused with a forest.

Shapes wear out their meaning
like jokes told several times
("Spouse of the boarder, down lexicon way").

I often forget what day it is
as light sweeps over the porch
and a hawk shadow crosses the field

to settle within some trees:
Harrier, Kestrel, Merlin.
And the sound of wind disturbs me.

Time is compacted in it,
insistently changing its manner.
I prefer the thought that nothing changes,

but even the rotting log
seen from the kitchen window
is turning to mushrooms and bugs—

it gives me the shivers, frankly.
How can people sit, as we saw yesterday,
in a tent of mosquito netting

while the wind lurches walls around them
like Catherine Deneuve in *Repulsion*
walking a breathing hall

with a rabbit in her purse?
I could never understand it.
Of course, if you're writing a poem,

some mortal symbolism might be of help,
launching a wave that never breaks
in an ocean you've had to construct.

4

"Dear Sir: I hope you'll consider reading
my book called *Reading Treasures*.
It consists of original words not like any other,

plus feelings and fantasies
none of which are true.
I'm also including pictures

that should give you Bare Ideas!
Keep them if you wish,
and as they fade through time

I hope you'll think of me
when the ambulance stalls in mental traffic
and percussion, pressure, and force

collide with homogenous light
in the rushing field and ether.
You give me money then?

But consider centripetal forceps.
The velocity of an average man
escaping a burning house

creates its own conventions not from
our arguments with ourselves but from
our arguments with the language,

which like the water imprisoned in rock
will steam out during discussion
yet not deflate the rock.

Perhaps Siam strong man?
The whirled and all its charms?
Supposing the laws of inertia,

the exertion of a finger
sends the perfect cart
over the perfect road

through the wilderness of Jack Skelley,
and a list of flashbacks occurs
in roughly the order they happened.

I'm glad you apprehend.
Both pink and circumspect,
with a sense of deep predation,

we sail toward Neonism, Gee Odes,
and Schuylerites, high on the quartz content.
Terrif! But topical, just so topical!

Dressed in polyester, how many have you,
horses? I have jump and flat.
In what sense do you think

Seurat's *Grande Jatte* is knowledge?
It's very understood,
no new ledge where to stand,

but important if it awes
or simply frames us there,
a smirk without its gods:

one thousand illustrations.
I hope you like my meaning and soon
will punish it. Yours in the pen, etc.''

5

Moths are covering windows,
though more sparsely than before.
I could turn out the lights

and watch them disappear,
but there's something appealing about them
as they strike the screen like fingers.

Today we saw the beaver pond
at the top of the hill,
its muddy lodge and sulfurous water.

Some call it Blueberry Hill,
both for the blueberries there
and for the lovers who visit,

but we weren't in that kind of mood.
The usual view was bluer, more fluorescent,
and none of us knew the names of trees,

so now I look through a book
containing Shadblows, Hawthorns,
and a kind of Prickly Ash

called the Toothache Tree.
It's the only northern citrus,
with berries that numb the palate,

and it often hosts the ''orange dog,''
a caterpillar, which, when excited,
emits the odor of rotting lemons.

I also look up Poplar (*Populus Tremuloides*).
Yesterday, pointing at one I'd liked,
a neighbor called it "junk."

Farmers will cut them like weeds,
but known as Trembling Aspens,
with thin white bark and leaves

that flash like spoons,
they're useful to the tourist.
Says Donald Culross Peattie,

"A breeze that is barely felt on the cheek
will send the foliage into a panic whisper."
Most of the day I slept, upset

by something mean I'd said.
All sentiment is ambition,
or so I've recently thought,

plus getting older gives me the present
a sentence at a time.
Flushed with that "success,"

I commit to memory the same old darkness
for which the dead are justly famous.
Here the land is never flat

between two dwindling towns.
Rain shrugs toward coasts
years and rivers later.

6

In the early morning when Joe gets up,
two herons are on the pond
eating the small brown trout.

Maybe nothing in nature is clumsy
until the moment it dies,
and we can't help watching that,

though to gawk is not to see,
if I understand Confucius.
It's character that counts.

But let's not dwell in truth.
It's delightful all around us,
therefore also gone,

and what are words to do
between a yes and yet?
They'll never change our lives,

so what did you expect?
And what did I think I wanted,
to be sadder and wiser, maybe?

On the other hand,
in the movie I watched last night
(A Midsummer Night's Dream),

Puck was played by Mickey Rooney
with hysteria and grandeur,
and Bottom was played by Cagney.

I loved their tragical mirth,
the ethereal voices
of tapdancing Maypole dancers

swirling in silk and darkness.
"Lead kindly, light"
is also a fine thing to hear

in the woods near a red farmhouse
with its family cemetery
exuding *memento mori.*

71

And so I go to sleep
in the midst of kindly nature,
my donkey head next to the princess.

7

I read today that Estée Lauder,
while having some ladies to tea,
made them stand on their heads in the garden

because they looked so sluggish,
and Magritte was so annoyed
when a stranger came to visit

he kicked him in the seat of his pants
then pretended nothing had happened.
When I feel anti-social,

I crawl into the carpet
with its memoir of spilled drinks,
so even when a lady places a card in my hand,

as she leaves with another man,
suggesting we meet by the sea,
I blush more from politeness

than from any lust I feel.
After a while, of course,
shyness loses its strict insistence

like an officer under fire,
and something like desperation
waves its little flag.

I mean, I think, what I'm saying.
Episodes pile up that will only embarrass me later
with breezy digressions in doubtful taste,

but at least the window is open—
you can turn your ear that way,
where civility is a bird announcing

how far its authority stretches.
Each new speculation is the story of self
both expansive and compressed.

You pretty well know the rest,
the "politesse de Durwood Kirby"
that is ours and ours alone.

So when ideas "happen,"
there's always a tent to pitch
on the windy slope of a notion.

As I wrote for Kenward today,
Bill's work is fully lighted
by the mind with its memory pressures

and by the "continuous present"
of the world outside the eye.
The dominoes fall in circles

with the clicking rush of tongues.
Feelings arrive as they will,
lived as they are imagined.

Refreshed from the rain-shaped pond
where a brat tossed a toad in the water
to see if it would float and the reeds

along the edge frightened everyone,
I begin to feel a lightness
running through my hands.

It's good you see right through me,
like the spoon in a glass of water
that bends toward the back of your head.

Each side of that amazement,
we're lover and fanatic,
having the same intentions

but different means and ends,
what was once remembered
and what remains to be seen.

From a Gazebo

Matins for some and curtains for
others. No birds sing. But then,
of course, it's fall. Birds don't
sing in the cold. They just go away,
and the wind strikes bricks and alleys
like office noise that keeps the
workers nervous or the struggles of
a sheep I found caught in a fence
and which, like Frank Sinatra, suavely
limped away. Yes, metaphor leads us
astray, to little lambs lost in the
woods and blue-eyed maidens waiting,
La Belle Dame and Daisy. But never
mind all that. Morning is sunny
and calm. The El train rumbles by,
eye-level with the window, though at
a repectable distance, so it's less
threat than art. Sometimes at night
it passes with its little panels
of light containing upright figures
like people in toy airplanes who
raise their shrieking hands. And
come to think of it, what must we
look like, framed in our night windows?
It's simply morning now, and somewhere
in its whiteness there is a shadowless
truth Plato might have liked. A truck
pulls up with beer, and two stout
gentlemen cart in ten red boxes with
"Stroh's" written on the sides. Steam
issues from a pipe: the laundromat
is open, where all the tough kids hang:
a city neighborhood where no one owns

a gazebo, and the prettiest thing one
sees is concrete when it rains. Oh,
dry and boring day, with my fever for
conquest unquenched, how can I go on
thinking? Have I said what saying
gives me, or am I in my mind, so notably
feeble in spite of querulousness that
suggests a kind of strength? (1. Knowledge
of subject matter   2. Written and oral
communication   3. Qualities of leadership
4. Dependability   5. Ability to plan
and organize   6. Relationships with others.
All of the above may be evaluated in
the following categories: Above Average,
Average, Below Average, Not Observed.
You may add additional pages if the
space provided does not prove sufficient.
Please sign your name at the bottom,
neither bluntly nor ornately.) I was
thinking, the other day, about a woman
I dated who later joined the Army. She'd
drag me off to Mass (fat chance of my
conversion) at Holy Name Cathedral
where Cardinals' hats are strung from the
ceiling. We like such quaint traditions
perhaps *because* they're passing, but
the hats don't seem to care whether
or not we care. They sway in the windy
cathedral. Caught in a bramble of
thought (that is, what was thought by
Scotus, Maritain) even a theologian
finds room for one more thought, bound
in its own tradition like a thousand
years of Latin. Matins, not midnight.
The gruesome matinee from which one
always emerges, surprised at the light
he finds. Morning stands for promise,
not sullen disappointment, so I lift

all spells of dread like scenery in
a play, and if I could sing with
heartbreaking tenor, I'd offer a song
to it. Aubade. The morning glory.

2

But that's not all. As our morning
song goes to pieces in a mist of
cigarettes, other flirtations occur,
though at a sparring distance. Koren
sobs at the window because her leaving
mother, with many things in mind, forgot
to turn and wave. Don't worry, kid,
she loves you. Hey, someone, come
around. Drop in. Have a ball. Let's
cut the rug sometime. Hey, you wanna
beer? Turn on the lights, it's dark.
Put on your old pink dress with the
deep decolletage and your fluffy
high-heeled slippers: we'll dance
to brittle records and hit the hot motel
with its sizzling bar and grill and
size-ten dance floor packed. For breakfast
I had some coffee, pecan coffee cake
(one sixteenth of it) and a glass of
orange juice made from concentrate.
The cake itself was sugar, pecan nuts,
non-fat milk and water, eggs, raisins,
salt, monoglycerides, yeast, dextrin,
artificial flavors, peanuts, walnuts,
calcium sulfate, sodium stearoyl
lactylate, potassium sorbate, spice
and coloring. Oh, yes, cottonseed oil.
It's terribly important. Say, isn't

this awfully droll? Who cares what's
in the cake? But I could feel your
interest as the list was being given.
Is he going to put "rat shit"? And you
derived some pleasure, however modest,
from the common details of life.
A lamp on during the day, especially
out of doors, is the kind of thing
I mean, or someone wearing mismatched
shoes, one high-heel and one ski boot.
But it needn't be that weird. A pebble
inside a Bible. Sun on a Panama hat.
My eyes rolling up in my head like
those statues on Rhodes which stood
looking out from niches. I'm made
from standing sand that's held up
by pure will, and even that is sifting.
Once I saw a movie in which a woman
held up a bottle of sand, exclaiming,
"It's from Los Alamos, the atom testing
site. It breeds by itself; every six
weeks or so, you got to dump some out.
It drifts inside the bottle." I was
thinking, too, of a man on television
who wears a beard of bees. He straps
the queen in a box just beneath his
chin, then workers and drones will
gather. The first bad thought and
he's dead, but he walks blithely around
and kisses his wife on the lips. She
has to put up with the guy. His whole
life's been these bees. They buzz
around his smile, nestle on the pillow.
The kids are used to Dad swarming in
his rocker: "What's on TV, kids?"
It's Mr. Moto or something: they mumble
what they say. Maybe the neighbors

grumble, but I say he's a hero—the man
is never nervous! Today I thought
it would snow, but it only rained, and
now at 3:21, while Koren is learning
to swim, bobbing ten feet deep, eyes
closed against the water, I end my little
dictation which grows like bottled sand.

3

The mind has sexes, too, and the
shifting from one to another is a
little like treading water with hands
held over your head. A parrot saying
"parrot." A blue chair on the veranda
(piazza, gallery) where Neruda rolls
with the girl on the seamless marble
slab, not in mystic pleasure but
gruntingly pounding each other through
blue serge, cotton, and lace. You, me,
us, them, we, our, nor, stare, collar,
holder, ivy, never, leisure, angle,
curfew, furlough, feather, eager—all
of it concerns, disabled, *déshabillé*.
But let me reassure you, in spite of
a French word heard, I've had my picture
taken with a decomposing group back
where clotheslines freeze, and my
farmboy bowl haircut still shapes the
way I stand with lyrical intentions
created from mud and desire (and an
average sense of relations) into nets
of words. It's nice being me, I imagine.
I accept the role with genial desperation.
My Desi Arnaz hair, James Dean crease

in the pants, Hermione Gingold manner,
Don Ameche teeth, Broderick Crawford
neck, and Jack Parr piercing look—
all lend a certain "don't know what"
to this gavotte of pedants and cynical
lack of events, as if we'd suddenly sunk
into Louisa's dream, neither oblique
nor elliptic, but directly terrified
by swimming horses and knives creating
bland traditions. I was born in Virginia
to modest professional parents. Religion
was part of our life. Used to mow the
lawn. Used to practice golf. Once
I saw a fox. (And here the memory fails,
as if a staggering man carrying a panel
crossed Hollywood and Vine between the
light and sight.) Kept from stern
elations by sterner weaknesses, one
chooses to live in the present, with
its counter suppositions like Jarvis
Liquor Stores. No nonfiction? No.
As Clausewitz once said, "War is
very simple, but it is also very
difficult." The same may be said
of life, that we love its deprivations,
so impeccably idiotic, that make us glad
for a sandwich and maybe cookies later.
My life consists of a shy acceptance
of just about everything—that is,
a sense of the worthless as having
a grim importance I can never equal:
a ball of string, for instance, that
gathers over the years, or dust growing
in a corner in roughly the shape
of a cat. Still, the reader gladly admits
admiring himself in the text, holding it
like a mirror so later he might say,

"That was me as a youth, careless
and contented, with adventure on my
mind," for the self is a topic that
never grows stale and nourishes like
bread. Even shattered glass expresses
gleeful Me to some marquise's child.
Still, it might be rather pleasant
to sit in simple quiet, my silence
only broken by certified nods of the
head, as I grow inwardly solid like
monuments taking shape. The sun goes
over twice, shadows spread and fade,
and pallidness is suggested by the
reader's "monastic" position as unicorn
attendant in a sweet medieval farce
not unlike television. The smuggest
view of life is yet unpioneered, and
though we're drawing closer, centuries
await with arrogance unimagined, rocking
out of cradles. Whatever we get said
won't turn the planet faster. The crowd
grows amorous as events on the ledge
take place, the weather of the language.

4

Koren sleeps on the floor because
there's nothing to watch, though she
might watch light from lamps or static
from the cat. Winter doldrums near:
the sky is grey today, though leaves
burn through, yellow, red, and orange
(it's nice they don't turn black) and
flowers remain just flowers in front
of the neighbor's house. Gardening's

a pleasure as one "intensifies," my
word for growing older. The radio
announcer on the Javanese Gamelan
Show says the piece we're hearing
is called "Neglected Plants." How
utterly nutty of him. The instrument
resembles a truck breaking down on
a road; I imagine red and yellow like
those in Costa Rica with little canary
bells that jostle with the ride. Both
aggressive and coy, the dash of a
scarf on a wall, it sounds so engagingly
noisy, but the real attraction lies
in how many people play it, whole
villages consorting in the merry,
ugly music broad as the thought of
a mile. I have a look for thinking,
a mask of concentration that serves
as well as words, though words are OK,
too. Gosh, I mean, like gee, their
glitzy mechanisms, the little springs
and whirrs of circling with outward
momentum the prey one self-creates.
Time is money (said). I have lots
of time. And there are lots of words,
even as topics narrow into single
"things," i.e., how you're feeling,
what didn't happen today, and more or
less how's the folks? The fog that
never lifted. The fever of trying
to mean when the slightest nod would
do—how noble is the speaker in his
very foolishness. Silence forever!
Prudence. Fueled by self-revulsion,
we practice our departure over cardboard
rocks and canvas-colored lakes, grimacing
with solutions in the midst of messes

made, for even the act of falling
is a generous exploration. (We land
in the room where we are with a knowledge
of all outdoors.) Last week I saw a
statue depicting Marsyas (who blew
from the flute such ravishing sounds
he was tempted to challenge Apollo)
in the midst of eating his beard,
in agonies of pretension. But the
crowd was more enthralled by a little
boy wrestling geese, a slight, libidinous
symbol of the kind that pees in fountains.
It was fun to walk around Calliope's
small breasts, an excavated muse.
(Uncover all of us later, and you'll
find us, hands in pockets, yawning
for all we're worth.) As for common
speech, how Marsyas must have cursed,
it's not just Nighttown slumming, but
rather the speaker's obsessions
cross-hatched in a pattern a long
black box with dials reveals as glyphs
on graphs. In the middle of all that
marble, I thought of my own nostalgia
for things that never happened, as
well as for things not said, how like
Marsyas I'd rather just eat my beard.
What's the way it is? Thelonious Monk,
with halts between the notes? A green
subliminal island? I'd like to say,
and rather directly, who cares about
that stuff? As for the matter of beauty,
I don't even know the names of flowers
beyond the dandelion—well, daisies,
violets, mums, carnations, gauche
birds of paradise and phallic ambrosial
things Maxine sometimes buys to fill

the house with sex. But what's a gentian?
Forsythia's probably yellow: that's
the end of it. Amaryllis, phlox, wisteria,
and bluet—I wouldn't know them from
blintzes, though I think I'm planting
gardenias when the sun lands on my hands
like that *Dark Victory* scene I watch
with maudlin tears every chance I get.
My mother in her thirties looked like
Bette Davis, except for the eyes, that is.
Now I'm off to bed. Goodnight, everyone.

5

What shall I think today? I can't
quote from Greek, don't know the names
of heroes whose weakness was their story.
But I know the work at hand, light touch
on the water, this broken-down typewriter
that can't even hold the margin. An instant
of the future slips into perception like
Dagwood's Mr. Dithers, and suddenly I
remember the honking of that horn
which I followed yesterday in a drunken,
empty rage and partly stupid bravado.
What if I caught the guy? Pound on
the roof of his car? Say, "Step out,
please, I want to scold you, sir"? One
mustn't act that way, so here's a solemn
vow that during the coming season I'll
keep my anger private and drink in
moderation. Today for lunch a burger,
French fries and a Coke. Maxine, though
she's eaten, joins me for some talk:
how dull the mail has been, what Koren

84

is doing at school. Should we have
another child? Now there's a topic
from which to swerve like one drunk
chasing another, but the answer, in short,
is yes. Meanwhile, it's decided, I'm
Raskolnikov as played by Robert Young.
Now the alphabet: Ask anemone. Bob,
the better bowler. Cyanide in cases.
Delapidated dairy. Eagerness enlarged.
Fragments of two friezes. Goy, Italian
style. High-school hotfoot haven.
Ignatius the Inexact. Jacquette,
Illinois. The Klondike Kut-up Show.
Breath of licorice on the girl I used
to kiss. Memoirs memorized. Necking
with the sheriff. *Oranges and Orangs*
by Elroy Rutabaga. The perilous periwinkle.
Quinine sipped in Teaneck. Residuals
from the series. Study hall in silk,
or how Miss Simpson dressed. The tidal
decomposure, not decomposition (that is,
nervous excitement) of the beach beneath
the pier. A tireless tour of Tours.
Uncle's elevation. The virtual extinction
of everything I believed: swine among
the pearls. Whales that beach themselves
like satchels on a platform. A Xerox
of my head, whirlpool ear repellent.
"Yes" to what you whispered as we drove
into the night. Zero on the test.

6

I have found a brief wing should
too much of weight the felt have who

be need must there for Souls some pleased
if plot of ground scant song's within
bound be to time twas moods past day
me hence for is and selves a twist
doom price we gloves to firm this high
bells fox by hour fair hair strong ants

bells peak near night for track undone
bloom soar that sell a bee's bent dance
loom wheel weaves wheel at maids nor pure
sift here her pens their blood serves four
cells she her mitts which are content
invent their sheiks past at not at fret nuns

7

Paul Hoover was born on April 30,
1946, first wave of the baby boom,
to Robert David Hoover, a pietistic
preacher who'd cry at the sight of
Ike (his sympathy was with history,
any large event, not the man himself:
tears at a parade of only a kid and
a dog) and Opal Catherine Shinaberry
(altered from Schoenberg). The nuclear
family Hoover lived in the Midwest,
though their manner and sense of
tradition were actually those of the
South, with talk of sweet potatoes,
fried chicken, collards, and kale.
The feel of the wheel of the '49
Oldsmobile that drove the Hoovers
(formerly Huber, farmer, umlaut over
"u") to church on Sunday morning after
baths on Saturday night. Thus time

efficiently and often sweetly passed.
A sampler on the wall contained a
smarmy prayer Flaubert would have loved,
not fleur-de-lis wallpaper but some
Dutch-uncle stuff: windmills, girls
in skirts, and oversize roses on a
blue background that seemed to breathe
in the night. Once, and only once,
was the radio ever played, and the
phonograph turned to rust, but TV
buzzed for days like flies in a corner
web. Young Hoover remembered sunlight
falling into the house, the eeking of
a screen, and sirens squeaking at noon,
not because of a fire, but just because
it was noon. In all of *Dr. Zhivago*,
the movie he saw twice, thinking it
high art, the chief thing that impressed
him was the thump of an iron on cloth.
He still had reason to wonder about
this young aesthete with the chic of
Field and Stream whose desire for
self-expression had the phobic width
of a billboard photograph, behind which,
he imagined, policemen started their
engines. The "self speech" of a tenor
who wants to sing Wagner like Verdi
instead of shouting it out like father
enraged at a candle. The absolute beauty
of a moist patch of grass on which glass
panels have fallen, which flattens it
to painting but still lets in the light.
(Be careful, by the way, where you step
in such conditions, for accidents usually
happen in or around the home, and even
a shoe too small can change the course
of a life. Pornography on ice, though at

first it sounds attractive, results in
nicks and burns. Aesthetically, too,
it hurts, as the grace of the skaters
collapses as other interests ensue.)
When Hoover went to a play, the pianist's
assistant, whose job was turning the pages
with the charm of a butler dancing, began
to quietly cry, moved by the show on stage.
As the music could not proceed, it turned
in quiet circles. Scenery fell on the
players as they scrambled to escape;
curtains went up when they shouldn't and
didn't come down when they should (painted
to look like bricks, they hung in folds
like curtains), and the amateur players
shrugged as if to say, "So what did you
expect?" A joyous presentation, for they
preferred the mistaken, medium awkwardness
with which their acting moved. And then,
another time, the way three bulky dancers
careened in being swans, the creaking
of the floor beneath galumphing feet,
and a little old lady, whose black top
hat matched her tux and cane, doing a sly
soft-shoe in a mix of innocence and raw
determination. Young Hoover considered
it all, life's complexities as they
pertain to art and art's inanities as
they derange a life, and settled on a
manner of determined noncommitment.
Some day, he'd figure this out. For now,
he was satisfied that nothing holds
together, which in itself is charming.
He left in laughing tears. If things
were totally clear, like spreading
circles of light, not dim as candled
eggs where shadow shapes appear, his

constant indiscretions might cease
as excitations, though probably not really.

8

The tinny music clatters, Elizabeth
Schwarzkopf again. Was she the only
one singing fifty years ago? It's a
plodding, dying dirge more notable for
its age than for its lyrical pomp. Then
a cheery beer-hall romp with martial
implications: boys, let's go to war!
Today is Veteran's Day. Let the VFW
have it, baked bean dinner parties,
American Legion bingo after white bread
snacks. An itchy ancient voice with
brassy coldness sings, "Pack up your
troubles in your old kit bag . . ."
That is, pioneers, wars will follow
depressions. So stick out your chests
with pride. It's life and all those
taxes for Rural Free Delivery and a
nuclear plant in your yard, glowing
phosphorent lettuce like poison left
out for the rats. But I digress from
the music which fades as the door
swings shut. Beauty should enfold me
in its cheap theatrical gown as a bat
enthralls a moth, but these are times
when several Marinettis spread like
stains on paper. Everyone wants to be
drums, sharp objects in the dark. It's
Berlin in the Eighties, and Warhol's doing
portraits for a little bit of money.
As John Singer Sargent said, the mouth's

where character's found: the sullen pout
and sensual purr or nervous hair-line
fractures that mean you're disappearing.
The morbid hesitation when the person
being drawn sees himself as victim:
"It's quite, uh, lovely, I think" (knowing
he's been skewered). The wicked look on
the painter's face as he packs you off
to history, having caught your soul,
diminished as it is, but you'll look good
on the wall as the party swirls below:
"That man on the countess's arm, was he
not the janitor's son before his profile
saved him? And Klosterman's candy fortune,
which has started to melt away, is it not
maintained by the studio he keeps?"
Ordinary life offers the better pleasures,
as Billy Rococo said, dumping the ashes
of Rico the Tenor in a soggy Jersey alley
verging on a swamp. It had been a terrible
day, filled with incidents (murder) that
made him question his human position.
But what to do with Rico, whose mordancy
had sustained him yet finally wouldn't
serve? Down the alley, tin cans clattered,
probably a cat. The night was clear and
crisp. A leaf, in the act of falling,
swerved to brush his cheek. Yes, life
was great in Jersey. He breathed, in his
satisfaction, a micromilligram of
polyphenyl chloride, and a light went
off in his eye. "Billy," she had
moaned as he flicked her hardened
nipple with the tip of his throbbing
tongue and pressed her quivering hand
to the rising knob in his pants.
Great waves, friction, ardor, caresses,

stays, and snaps. Her warmth had now
enclosed him. It felt, it felt, so good!
"Rococo" was carefully written above
the front door bell of the house on
Paradise Parkway. "Welcome," said
the doormat. "Rico," she said to the box
containing Rico's ashes, "Rico, speak
to me!" But Rico's time had passed,
and now the wind blew down, scattering
everything into the swamp and beyond.

9

But let this make a world, as single
words can do: Sundays, Easter, Tuesdays
in Spring, Bank Holidays in Summer,
Christmas Day and Boxing Day, New
Year's, Easter Eve, and May Day.
Bill Atkins, Vincent Carter, Clifford
and Eddie Johnson, Art Hoyle, Danny
Barber, George Bean, Edwin Williams,
Bill Porter, Willie Pickens, Ron Kolber,
and Steve Barry. The Landslide.
The Condor. The Rescue of Robert.
The Open Sea. The Whale. Platform
and Ladder. Old Bad Money. Blureed.
River. Rooves. A Donkey Ride in the
Dunes. Glove, groin, fever, chimney.
Reading *Perspectives in Poultry*. Sunday,
Monday, Tuesday, Wednesday, Thursday,
Friday, Saturday, Sunday, Monday,
Tuesday, Wednesday. Diesel, feather,
clinger. Blond, backseat, drizzle.
Fetlock, padlock, thumbnail, mirror.
A slum. A cloud. A home. Closet,

creche, recess, bowl. Why are fish
not given to fevers? Why are animals
soft in youth? What part of water
is more truly water, the bottom, top,
or middle? Why are fools so fond of
cheese? January, February, March,
April, May, June, July, August,
September, October, November, December.
Je suis le bon berger. Blanc comme
la neige. C'est moi qui vous console.
Man with tuba. Man in parade. The
giveaway, the false confession, a
mistletoe kiss on lips. "In answer
to your question, yes, I'm feeling
better, in spite of the fog in my
bones and delapidated spirit like
soiled wallpaper. Things are clearly
improving for Bobby, me, and the dog,
but neighbors keep a standard of
ruthless censorship that makes the soul
feel soggy. Yours in penitence,
Prudence." So Puritans *do* lurk in
the almost modern conscience. We're
figures on a landscape sectioned by
strict hedges, which, even when they
flower, shuttle us off to a corner.
To put it another way:

The Pilgrim's foot

dreamed a ladder

May 16, 1950

Dear Grandmother

how is the college

from all the guys

        to all the gods

Here's the train

        to Upper Tooting

failed designs

        for a new triangle

hermetic signs

        of a new melancholy

Mr. Swinburne

        stalled in traffic

the glory of leaving

        your pants unzipped

maliciously small

        American music

egg-shaped marks

        on flattened grass

the new magi

        the new spoonbenders

Candy Bangs

Just Plain Beauty

antique seas

and modern water

schoolbells ring

and children sing it's

mother knows for

children's clothes it's

Jacob Epstein

William Blake

Nobody knows

the trouble I've seen

confusing aesthetic

with surgery

the dog that gnaws

on saxophones

J.D. McClatchy

teaching at Yale

whose final lecture

"Ballistics and Dancing"

when Amos Alonzo

       was a verb

lyric filler

       "satin and vacant"

a man of meat

       a piece of dreams

Demosthenes

       the letter "R"

shadows standing

       in the shade

not for profit

       Mendeleyev

the swarm contracts

       round perfect trees

10

Dear Maxine: Thanks for sending
the magazine and book. Glad to have
them both. Wish I could reciprocate
with something new of my own. Enjoyed
meeting you. Remember many years ago

calling one time from Connolly's on
Devon (no longer Connolly's) to see
if you felt like coming out, but there
was no answer. Even enjoyed addressing
this to Jarvis. Used to call it Nervous
Jarvis when I lived there—13 something,
a courtyard building by alley. That's
another story. Hello to Paul. Best, Stuart.

Dear Stuart: Years ago, when you wrote
about Peter's book, I was angry with you.
How could you hate such beauty? Indeed,
I ask you now. For years I didn't write you,
but followed your career, resenting your
success. Now Peter has subsided, and we
stand as survivors, and while I still
defend him, I wish you the best and thanks.
Tonight we dine with friends whose policies
have changed from *succès de scandale* to
tradition, form, and craft. Afterwards,
a movie, something by Roger Corman as
cheap and overripe as our image of ourselves,
which gradually we're perfecting so others
may believe. My doubt shows on my face,
reversals and inversions that won't disguise
themselves, like gross banana slugs. But what
a nightmare thought! Joyce, I read today,
lived on Via Scussa. Does that mean Road
of Pardons? I hope you'll pardon me. Paul.

II

The lesser scoup is both a duck and a
sequence of events moving on the pond
where millions of water bugs are lurching

in circles like conjuring hands. Home runs
are events, dresses painted blue, and any
location, minus its wind, is there to be seen
if not to be hit. Its name is an event:
Grinder's Grove, Joe Island, Atlanta, Tantrum,
Gratis, and Reckless, Oklahoma. And then
there's Chagrin Falls: one wonders how
it happened. Some things never happen
but keep on happening: the weather,
how one talks, the attitudes of sharks
in warm or warmer water. And sentences
are events: "The cat sits on the mat"
and "Yeats, in search of a frame of character,
concerned himself a good deal with the dead
because their fundamental rhythms could be
determined." I put a ball on the table.
It is white and firm. It does not roll,
metaphors no moon, is not required of its
setting. Hostility from corners, snow
at the "anxious" window, for we often make
events where they refused to be, and in
a certain light we are events ourselves,
hogging center stage. When philosophers
go out to eat, we see how dizzy they get
watching milk descend from a pitcher to
the glass, accounting for its whiteness
by ignoring the darkness in it, where thousands
of events surpass their recognition. They
mark a point where the first drop lands
and build a shrine to it, while the last
drops away into what it is with such coercive
ease that they think a thing has happened.

The work is fashioning, being fashioned
by the work—it sounds like "fastened,"
drunk. You've been depressed at noon,
pleased at two o'clock, run toward lights
of cars, slept in clean motels, mumbled
underground, done back flips from wedding
cakes where you were posed as groom.
The land is flat as you can stand, with
a dip in the road for a valley and rain
that shrugs toward coasts years and rivers
later. But a joy in your possession
insistently provokes like two within the
choir preferring other songs. It's a
meager tourist town where most of the
cabins are shuttered and paddle boats
are filled with snow no one could have
imagined under American heaven. Now they're
too heavy to move beside a quiet lake
frozen like a road, and the citizens,
whoever they are, must be sleeping in
for streets to be so empty at noon on a
winter Tuesday. Population: four. Only
your insistence might turn them out of doors
to pose for a picture together, but they
stay locked in smiles, inert anecdotes.
You might fashion them the way a child
draws mountains with blue chalk and some
haste, but they shake at your attentions
and even seem to say, "Please leave us
alone; kindly go away." Their world remains
itself, shaped like snow that falls on
rocks and walls without your intervention.

THE FIGURES

Rae Armantrout *Extremities* $2.50
Paul Auster *Wall Writing* $3.00
David Benedetti *Nictitating Membrane* $3.00
Steve Benson *As Is* $5.00
Alan Bernheimer *Cafe Isotope* $3.00
John Brandi *Diary from a Journey to the Middle of the World* $4.00
Summer Brenner *From the Heart to the Center* $3.00
Summer Brenner *The Soft Room* $4.00
David Bromige *My Poetry* $6.00
Laura Chester *My Pleasure* $3.00
Laura Chester *Watermark* $4.00
Tom Clark *Baseball* $6.50
Clark Coolidge *The Crystal Text* $10.00
Clark Coolidge *Melencolia* $3.50
Clark Coolidge *Mine: The One That Enters the Stories* $7.50
Michael Davidson *The Prose of Fact* $5.00
Lydia Davis *Story and Other Stories* $5.00
Christopher Dewdney *Spring Trances in the Control Emerald Night
        & The Cenozoic Asylum* $5.00
Johanna Drucker *Italy* $3.50
Barbara Einzig *Disappearing Work* $4.00
Norman Fischer *On Whether or Not to Believe In Your Mind* $7.50
Kathleen Fraser *Each Next* $4.00
Gloria Frym *Back to Forth* $4.00
Merrill Gilfillan *River Through Rivertown* $4.00
Lyn Hejinian *Writing is an Aid to Memory* $4.00
Paul Hoover *Idea* $7.50
Fanny Howe *Introduction to the World* $5.00
Bob Perelman *a.k.a.* $5.00
Bob Perelman *The First World* $5.00
Bob Perelman *7 Works* $3.50
Tom Raworth *Tottering State* $11.50
Tom Raworth *Writing* $10.00
Stan Rice *Some Lamb* $4.00
Kit Robinson *Down and Back* $3.00
Stephen Rodefer *The Bell Clerk's Tears Keep Flowing* $12.00 (Cloth)
Stephen Rodefer *Four Lectures* $7.50
James Schuyler *Early in '71* $2.00
Ron Silliman *Tjanting* $10.00
Julia Vose *Moved Out on the Inside* $4.00
Guy Williams *Selected Works 1876-1982* With an Essay
        by Gus Blaisdell $10.00
Geoffrey Young *Subject to Fits* $5.00